From Your Friends At **The MAILBOX®**

APRIL

A MONTH OF REPRODUCIBLES AT YOUR FINGERTIPS!

Grade 1

Editor:
Susan Hohbach Walker

Writers:
Catherine Broome, Amy Erickson, Sharon Murphy,
Susan Hohbach Walker, Kimberly Wombough

Art Coordinator:
Clevell Harris

Artists:
Nick Greenwood, Clevell Harris,
Rob Mayworth,
Kimberly Richard, Barry Slate

Cover Artist:
Jennifer Tipton Bennett

www.themailbox.com

©1998 by THE EDUCATION CENTER, INC.
All rights reserved.
ISBN #1-56234-224-X

Manufactured in the United States
10 9 8 7 6 5 4

Table Of Contents

Name _____

April Calendar Capers

Monday	Tuesday	Wednesday	Thursday	Friday
April 1 is April Fools' Day. Invite students to tell their favorite jokes.	April 2 commemorates the birthday of Hans Christian Andersen, author of more than 150 fairy tales. Read aloud some of his delightful stories.	National Library Week is celebrated in April. Have each student make a list of his three favorite books.	The first modern Olympic® Games had nine sports and were held on April 6, 1896, in Greece. Ask students to choose the sporting event they would most like to enter.	April 7 is World Health Day. Encourage students to make posters promoting good health habits.
Astronomy Day is observed between mid-April and mid-May. Ask each child to write a story about a shooting star.	April is National Garden Month. Have students name three of their favorite foods that come from gardens.	April 14 is Pan American Day. Show students North and South America on a map.	The eraser was invented on April 15, 1770. Challenge each child to keep track of how many times she uses her eraser today.	On April 16 celebrate the birthday of film star Charlie Chaplin. Invite students to perform funny scenes without talking.
April is Prevention Of Animal Cruelty Month. Brainstorm with students ways they can help animals.	Ask students to draw three signs of spring.	April is National Automobile Month. Have each student design a car he'd like to drive in the future.	Public Schools Week is celebrated in April. Ask students to list six ways their lives would be different if they did not attend school.	April is National Humor Month. Explain to students the meaning of the saying "Laughter is the best medicine." Ha Ha Ha Ha Ha Ha Ha
Recognize Earth Day on April 22 by reading aloud *For The Love Of Our Earth* by P. K. Hallinan (Ideals Children's Books, 1992).	Have students paint rainbows with watercolors.	In honor of Fresh Florida Tomato Month, ask students to brainstorm foods that contain tomatoes.	Celebrate National Honesty Day on April 30. Discuss with students the saying "Honesty is the best policy." HONESTY	In most states, National Arbor Day is held the last Friday in April. Take your students outside to sit under a tree as you share Shel Silverstein's *The Giving Tree* (Lectorum Publications, Inc.; 1996).

Eat Fruits And Vegetables Every Day!

©1998 The Education Center, Inc. • *April Monthly Reproducibles* • Grade 1 • TEC948

Note To The Teacher: Highlight special days and events with these fact-filled ideas.

3

Name _____

April
Events And Activities For The Family

Directions: Select at least one activity below to complete as a family by the end of April. *(Challenge: See if your family can complete all three activities.)*

The ABCs Of Spring

Celebrate the arrival of spring with this letter-perfect idea! Brainstorm with your child things associated with this season. Then invite a family member to name a spring word or phrase that begins with *A,* such as "afternoons in the park" or "April showers." Continue with the remaining letters of the alphabet by having each family member, in turn, name the next letter and a corresponding seasonal word or phrase. From *A* to *Z,* this vocabulary-building activity is sure to please!

Astronomy Day

Recognize Astronomy Day with a project that's out of this world! Astronomy Day is observed on a Saturday near the first quarter moon between mid-April and mid-May. On or near this special day, have your child create a crayon-resist painting of outer space. To begin, he or she colors a space scene with broad heavy strokes on white construction paper. Then the child paints over the entire picture with black watercolor paint. (The crayon wax will resist the paint.) Allow the painting to dry; then display it for your entire family to enjoy. No doubt your youngster will have a galaxy of fun creating this star-studded scene!

Royal Retellings

Hans Christian Andersen, author of more than 150 fairy tales, was born on April 2, 1805. When he was a child, he spent many hours listening to folktales and making puppets to act out plays. Invite your child to do the same! First read aloud some of Andersen's delightful fairy tales (see "Recommended Literature" on this page). Then help your child use white construction paper, crayons, scissors, tape, and craft sticks to make stick puppets of characters from your child's favorite fairy tale. Reminding your child to include the beginning, middle, and end of the story, have him or her use the completed puppets to retell the fairy tale in his or her own words. With these princely puppets, story retelling will be a royal treat!

Recommended Literature

The Emperor's New Clothes retold by Anthea Bell and illustrated by Dorothee Duntze (North-South Books Inc., 1997)

The Red Shoes retold and illustrated by Barbara Bazilian (Whispering Coyote Press, 1997)

The Ugly Duckling illustrated by Lisa McCue (Western Publishing Company, Inc.; 1995)

Note To The Teacher: Distribute one copy of this reproducible to each student at the beginning of the month. Encourage each family

to complete at least one activity by the end of April.

Plip, Plop, Raindrops

As the saying goes, "April showers bring May flowers." So what better time to focus on the refreshing properties of rain. Whether or not you're experiencing April showers in your community, you'll enjoy sprinkling your curriculum with this roundup of rainy-day reproducibles.

Sounds Like Rain

Have you ever stopped to listen to a rainstorm? From its first drip-drop sounds to the roar of a downpour, there are many sounds to be heard. If you experience a rainstorm at school, have your students stop to listen to the different sounds the rain makes. If possible, stand under a covered area outdoors or open classroom windows for better listening. Back in your classroom, invite students to create sounds that imitate rainfall. (For example, you might have all of your students snapping their fingers at once to sound like sprinkling rain. Quickly stomping their feet will create a roaring downpour.) Follow up the experience by asking each child to write a poem titled "Sounds Like Rain" using their favorite rainy words. (See Rainy Writing on this page.)

rain

rainy

drip

drop

water

wet

raindrop

splish-splash

sprinkle

downpour

umbrella

pitter-patter

cloud

puddle

weather

storm

shower

Rainy Writing

Give your students a boost when writing about rainy topics by creating this special word wall specifically for rain-related words. Write each word on a separate raindrop cutout and display each cutout on a decorative bulletin board. Don't forget to add your own favorites to the list. For added appeal, display an umbrella or an umbrella cutout near your bulletin board. Now when students are asked to write an original rain-related story or poem, they can refer to this collection of words.

Name_____

A Week's Worth Of Rain

It has rained for five days.
A **rain gauge** measured the rainfall
each day.

Monday	Tuesday	Wednesday	Thursday	Friday
6 5 4 3 2 1 inches	6 5 4 3 2 1 inches	6 5 4 3 2 1 inches	6 5 4 3 2 1 inches	6 5 4 3 2 1 inches

Write or circle to answer each question. Use the graph.

1. On what day did it rain the most? _____

2. How many inches of rain fell on Friday?
   4 inches   5 inches   6 inches

3. Which day got more rain than Monday, but less rain than
   Friday? _____

4. Which day got the least amount of rain?
   Monday   Wednesday   Friday

5. Which two days got the same amount of rain?

   _____ and _____

6. How much rain fell during all five days? _____ inches

Note To The Teacher: To extend this lesson, measure your local rainfall for one week. Create your own graph based on the results.

Rainy-Day Words

Count the letters in each word.
Write each word in a space where it fits.

3 letters
wet

4 letters
drop
mist

5 letters
rainy

6 letters
shower ✓

7 letters
drizzle

8 letters
downpour
sprinkle

Write each ⬤ letter.

Unscramble the letters to find out what rain makes. Write.

_____

Name _____

Puddle Practice

Add.
Glue each raindrop above its sum.
Glue the extra raindrop on the back of this sheet.
Write the sum.

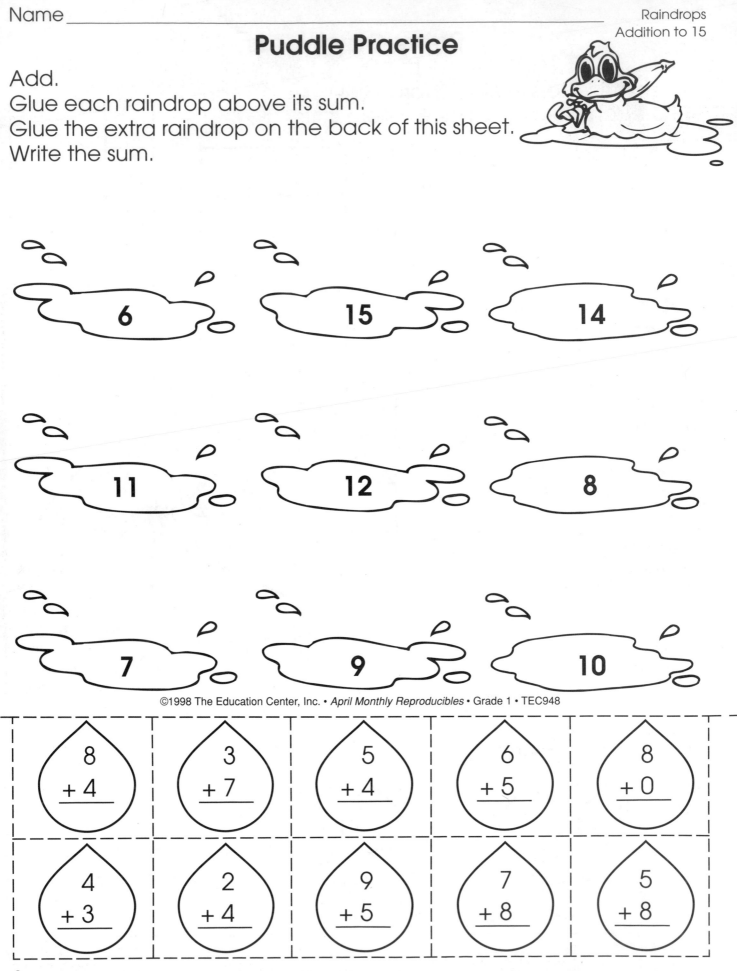

6   15   14

11   12   8

7   9   10

$$8 + 4$$ $$3 + 7$$ $$5 + 4$$ $$6 + 5$$ $$8 + 0$$

$$4 + 3$$ $$2 + 4$$ $$9 + 5$$ $$7 + 8$$ $$5 + 8$$

RAINBOWS

Brimming with brilliant color, there's nothing like a rainbow to brighten up the sky after a rain. Since April is famous for rain showers, your chance of seeing rainbows this month could be high. So treat your students to a journey into the realm of rainbows with these colorful activities.

Rainbow Research

The best way to study rainbows is to create one so your students can examine the range of colors. Tilt a mirror in a shallow pan of water; then set it so that direct sunlight hits the mirror. A rainbow will appear on a nearby wall. If you have access to a triangular prism, you can hold that in the sunlight to create the same effect. Rounding up rainbows will be a snap with these simple techniques.

Rainbow Relay

Reinforce the order of a rainbow's colors with this fun race. Line up three or four sets of six children each at a starting line. For each group, give each child a different-colored "crown" (made from a 5 1/2" x 18" sheet of construction paper) in the following colors: red, orange, yellow, green, blue, purple. On a signal, have the "red" child from each group run to a turning mark and then return to his starting position. At that point, have each group's "red" student pick up the "orange" student by holding her hand. The two children then run and touch their turning point before returning to their group. At that point the "yellow" child from each group holds the "orange" child's hand and the three make the trip again. Have each group continue this pattern, adding "green," "blue," and "purple" on each of the return trips. By the last leg, you'll have a rainbow of students in each group racing to be the most rapid rainbow!

Name_____

Rainbow Delight

Write > or < between each pair of clouds.
The first one has been done for you.

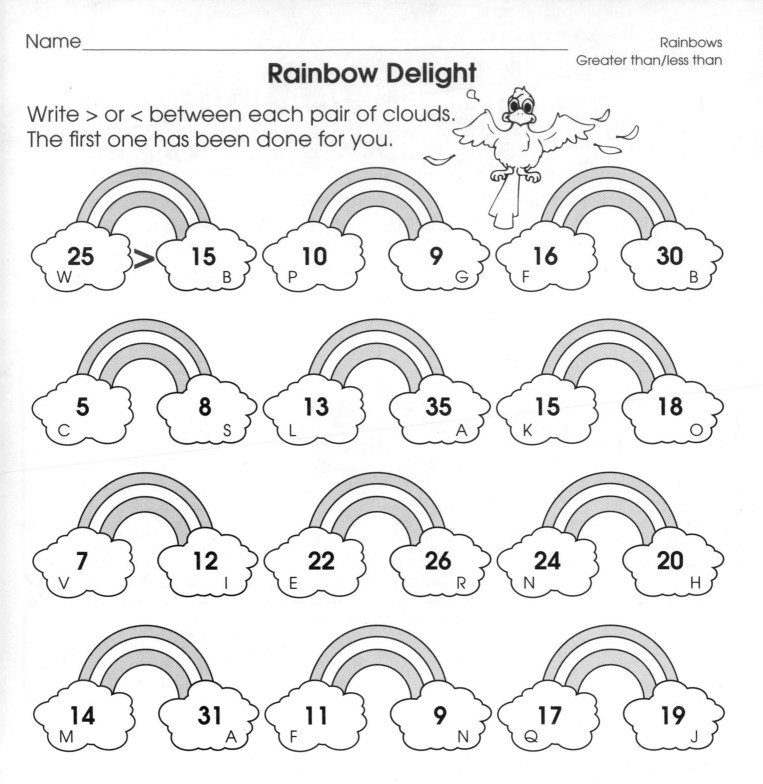

| 25 > 15 | 10   9 | 16   30 |
| W   B | P   G | F   B |

| 5   8 | 13   35 | 15   18 |
| C   S | L   A | K   O |

| 7   12 | 22   26 | 24   20 |
| V   I | E   R | N   H |

| 14   31 | 11   9 | 17   19 |
| M   A | F   N | Q   J |

To solve the riddle, match the letters of the greater numbers to the lines.
Some numbers will not be used.

What kind of bow is hard to tie?

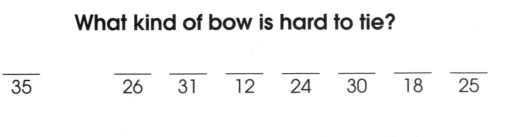

____ ____ ____ ____ ____ ____ ____ ____
 35   26   31   12   24   30   18   25

Name _____

Read the poem.

Looking At Rainbows

Red, orange, yellow, and green,
These are some of the colors I've seen.
Now I see blue and purple, I think.
Do rainbows have the color pink?

Follow each direction. Use the poem.

1. Write six color words.

_____   _____

_____   _____

_____   _____

2. Write two rhyming words.

_____   _____

3. Write the title of the poem.

_____

4. Count the lines in this poem. Write the number.

_____

Bonus Box: On the back of this sheet, write about the color pink.
Do you think pink is a color in rainbows? Why or why not?

Name

Colorful Clouds

Color each cloud that has two equal parts.

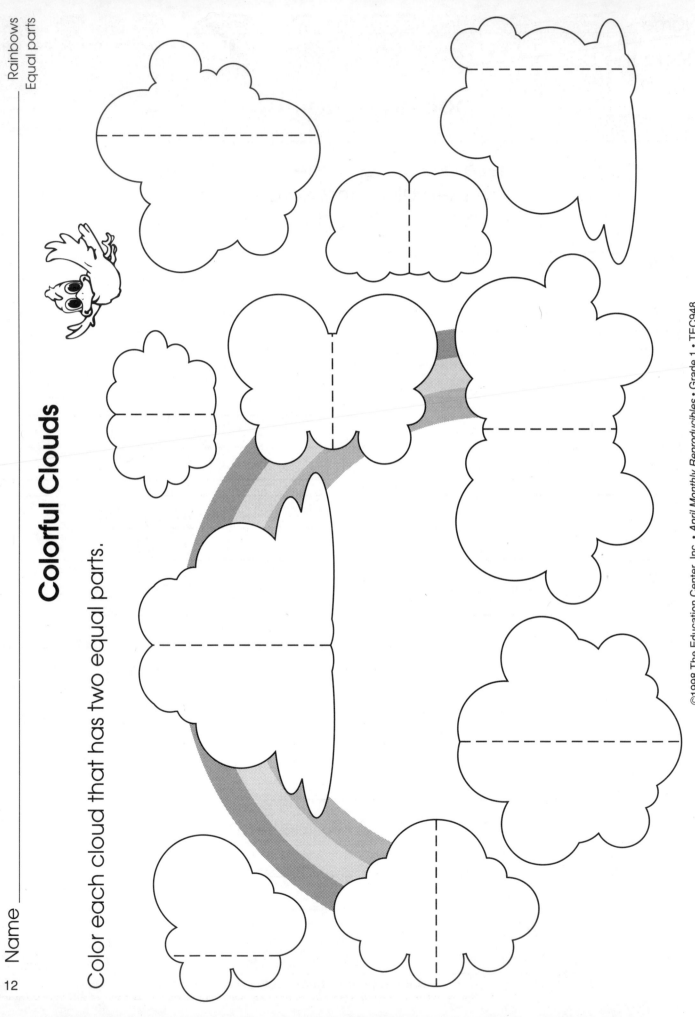

Earth Day, first celebrated on April 22, 1970, is observed to remind us of the importance of preserving the natural resources in our environment. This day calls attention to the needs of protecting clean water, healthy trees, and fresh air. It also calls for a commitment to cleaning up any pollution, litter, or other environmental problems.

Recycle Fair

Try this fun family project to celebrate Earth Day. Ask each child to make a toy, a useful machine, or another original invention completely from recycled products. For best results, ask each child to complete the assignment at home with the help of her family. Designate a day for the finished projects to be brought to school; then set up a display in your classroom or another area of your school. Invite school personnel, other classes, and students' friends or family members to attend the viewing. Encourage each child to stay near her project to demonstrate it or answer questions posed by the visitors. This is sure to get rave reviews from all who attend and participate.

Water Waste

Water—a resource taken for granted—plays an enormous role in our everyday lives. It's so simple these days to turn on the faucet and simply let this resource wash away. How can you and your students help to preserve water? It's simpler than you might think. Share these bits of trivia and water-saving efforts with your students.

- Turn off the water while you brush your teeth. Up to nine gallons of water could be wasted if you don't!
- Put a bottle of water in your refrigerator to cool. When you need a refreshing drink, you won't have to let the water run while you wait for cold water. As much as three gallons could be wasted if you wait for cold tap water.
- If you're going to take a bath, plug the tub right away so you won't waste any water.
- If you do have to let tap water run, capture it in a container and water a thirsty houseplant.

Name _____

Paper By The Piece

Count.
Record your results.

	Monday	Tuesday	Wednesday	Thursday	Friday
85					
80					
75					
70					
65					
60					
55					
50					
45					
40					
35					
30					
25					
20					
15					
10					
5					
0					

Solve and write.
How many sheets of paper were recycled for all five days?

_____ sheets

- -

Note To The Teacher: Set up a collection box for used paper. At the end of each day, have students count the number of sheets,
14   record it on this graph, and remove the paper from the box. Repeat for the remaining days.

Name_____

All For Earth

Check the items that are recycled at
this recycling plant.

☐ newspaper

☐ aluminum cans   ☐ phone books

☐ tin cans   ☐ magazines

☐ glass   ☐ cardboard

☐ other _____

_____

Write the answer to each question.

1. How do the materials get here? _____

_____

2. What do the recycled materials become? _____

_____

_____

3. What would happen to these items if they weren't recycled

here? _____

_____

_____

4. How can I help recycle? _____

_____

Note To The Teacher: If possible take your class to a recycling plant. Have each child complete this survey during the trip. If a trip is
not possible, call a local recycling center to obtain this information. Have each child complete the survey during a class discussion. 15

Put In A Good Word

Earth needs our care. For each beginning letter, write a kind word
   to describe Earth.
Cut.

Name

_____

E _____

A _____

R _____

T _____

H _____

Note To The Teacher: Display the completed cutouts on a bulletin board with the title "Our Important Earth."

From Another World

Imagine that you live on a make-believe planet. It is very different from Earth. Think about Earth; then write a story about your new planet. Describe how life is different.

_____

_ _

_____

_ _

_____

_ _

_____

_ _

_____

_ _

_____

_ _

_____

_ _

_____

_ _

_____

Earth-Wise Ways

Color each picture that shows a way to help the earth.

TREES ARE TOPS!

What better way to celebrate spring and Arbor Day than with a study of trees? Trees are honored by most states in April or May on Arbor Day. This holiday originated on April 10, 1872, as a result of Julius Sterling Morton's efforts to bring recognition to the value of trees. This Nebraskan newspaper publisher promoted planting trees because they benefited the environment. Complement your discussion about this important holiday by sharing these "tree-rific" facts with students:

- The Traveler's-Tree of Madagascar holds up to one pint of water inside each of its leaf stalks, providing travelers with drinking water.
- The Montezuma baldcypress in Mexico has the thickest tree trunk. It has a diameter of over 40'.
- The Ombu tree of Argentina is one of the hardiest trees. The tree's wood is so moist that it will not burn, and it is so spongy that it cannot be cut.
- Baobab trees store water in their trunks. When the tree gets water from the trunk in dry weather, the trunk becomes noticeably thinner.
- Sequoias are among the tallest trees in the world. Some are more than 300' tall.

Amazing Trees

"Wood" you believe that a baseball bat, a cereal box, rubber gloves, and a chocolate bar have something in common? Each of them is made from trees! Wood, paper, rubber, and food are some of the many types of products that come from trees. Collect sample items from each of these categories and show them to students. Explain that trees are valuable to us because they are a source for each of these items. On a large sheet of paper, make a chart with these headings: wood, paper, rubber, and food. Title the chart "Tree Products." Challenge each youngster to bring a small item from home that came from a tree. Have him show the class his item and tell in which category it belongs. Write the name of the item in the appropriate column on the chart. As the lists grow, students' appreciation of trees will grow too!

A Bushel Of Facts

This "tree-mendous" display will be the pick of the crop! In advance mount a large tree shape on a brightly colored bulletin board and make several tagboard apple stencils. Place the stencils, red paper, pencils, and scissors in a center. During your study of trees, have each youngster visit the center, trace a stencil on red paper, and cut out the resulting apple shape. Then direct him to write a fact about trees on his apple and place it in a bushel basket near the bulletin board. At a designated time each day, take the apples from the basket, read and discuss the facts with students, and post the apples on the tree. No doubt a lot of learning will take root with this "a-peel-ing" activity!

Tree Products			
Wood	**Paper**	**Rubber**	**Food**
baseball bat	cereal box	rubber gloves	chocolate
frame	magazine	rubber bands	allspice
blocks	paper towels		apple
paintbrush handle	books		walnuts

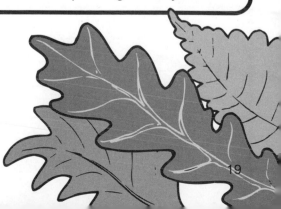

The Parts Of A Tree

Read.

A tree has one stem called a trunk. Bark covers the trunk and branches. Bark is a tree's skin. The leaves on a tree make food for it. The branches and leaves together are called the crown. Roots hold a tree in place.

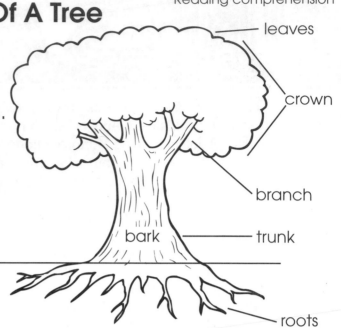

leaves

crown

branch

bark — trunk

roots

**Read the questions.
Write the answers on the lines.**

1. How many stems does a tree have?

_____

_____

2. What is a tree's skin called?

_____

_____

3. What makes food for a tree?

_____

_____

4. What holds a tree in place?

_____

_____

5. What are four parts of a tree?

_____   _____

_____   _____

_____   _____

_____   _____

Name _____

A Tree's Year

Cut and glue to match each season.
Draw a picture for each season.

Spring	Summer	Fall	Winter

Bonus Box: What is your favorite season? Write about it on the back of this sheet.

©1998 The Education Center, Inc. • *April Monthly Reproducibles* • Grade 1 • TEC948

The tree has many leaves.	Buds grow on the tree.	The branches are bare.	The leaves fall off the tree.

Note To The Teacher: Introduce this lesson by reading aloud *The Seasons Of Arnold's Apple Tree* by Gail Gibbons (Harcourt Brace & Company, 1988) or *A Busy Year* by Leo Lionni (Alfred A. Knopf Books For Young Readers, 1992).

Name_____

Fact Family Tree

Write each answer.

6 + 7 = _____

7 + 6 = _____

13 – 6 = _____

13 – 7 = _____

9 + 7 = _____

7 + 9 = _____

16 – 9 = _____

16 – 7 = _____

4 + 8 = _____

8 + 4 = _____

12 – 4 = _____

12 – 8 = _____

8 + 7 = _____

7 + 8 = _____

15 – 7 = _____

15 – 8 = _____

5 + 7 = _____

7 + 5 = _____

12 – 5 = _____

12 – 7 = _____

Bonus Box: On the back of this sheet, write four facts for this number family: 5, 6, 11.

Name _____

Trees Are Terrific!

Write the words in order to make sentences.
Add punctuation.

comes   Wood   trees   from

1. in   live   Animals   trees

_ _

2. us   shade   give   Trees

_ _

3. on   trees   grow   Fruits

_ _

4. paper   make   trees   from   We

_ _

5.

Bonus Box: What is made with wood? On the back of this sheet, write as many things as you can.

Leafy Problems

Subtract. Write each answer.
Color a leaf with the matching number.

9

8

13	14	16	12
− 6	− 5	− 8	− 9

5

6

12	17	15	12
− 6	− 9	− 9	− 5

3

9

14	18	13	12
− 7	− 9	− 5	− 3

7

7

17	14	15	16
− 8	− 9	− 6	− 9

6

8

Bonus Box: There are 18 leaves on a tree. Nine fall off. How many are left?
Write the answer on the back of this sheet.

8   **9**   **7**   **9**   **7**   **9**

JELLY BEAN JAMBOREE

Whet students' appetites for learning fun with this tempting jelly bean unit! Jelly beans of all colors and flavors have been popular snacks since their invention in the 1800s. These sugary treats are made using a process called *panning*. During this process, the center of the candy (a mixture of water, cornstarch, sugar, corn syrup, and flavorings) is placed in a rotating pan and sprayed with flavored and colored syrups. Repeated coatings form the candy's outer shell. There are many different flavors of jelly beans, including cinnamon, lemon, and coconut.

In 1980 the Jelly Belly® blueberry jelly bean was invented in honor of Ronald Reagan's inauguration; three-and-a-half tons of red, white, and blue jelly beans were sent to Washington, D.C.!

President Reagan arranged to have jelly beans sent into space for the astronauts aboard the space shuttle *Challenger* in 1983.

Fair Share

This beginning division activity will be a sweet success! To start, read aloud *The Doorbell Rang* by Pat Hutchins (Mulberry Books, 1989). At the conclusion of this predictable story, discuss with students how the number of cookies each child received changed as more visitors arrived. Then give each student a copy of page 26 and ask him to color and cut out the jelly beans at the bottom of his sheet. Have each youngster use the resulting counters and the jars pictured to model and solve each problem. Instruct each student to share the jelly beans equally for each problem and to write his answers on the lines provided. For an added challenge, ask each child to complete the Bonus Box problem. If desired conclude this appetizing lesson with a yummy snack of jelly beans—shared equally, of course!

LATEST AND GREATEST JELLY BEAN FLAVORS

candy cane   hot dog   ice cream

pepperoni pizza   marshmallow   chocolate chip

Tasty Titles

The Incredible Jelly Bean Day by Taylor Maw (Landmark Editions, Inc.; 1997)
Jelly Beans For Sale by Bruce McMillan (Scholastic Inc., 1996)

Flavorful Fun

Tantalize students' taste buds with this creative activity! First provide a variety of jelly beans for youngsters to sample. Discuss with children the relationship between the colors and flavors of the jelly beans. Have each youngster name her favorite kind of jelly bean and explain why it appeals to her. Then challenge each student to invent a new flavor of jelly bean, choose a corresponding color for it, and create a poster promoting it. Invite each youngster to advertise her new flavor by sharing her completed poster with classmates. No doubt students will eat up this imagination-boosting lesson!

Fair Share

Listen and do.

2 people 6 jelly beans How many does each person get? ____	2 people 12 jelly beans How many does each person get? ____
2 people 10 jelly beans How many does each person get? ____	2 people 8 jelly beans How many does each person get? ____

2 people 4 jelly beans How many does each person get? ____
2 people 14 jelly beans How many does each person get? ____

Bonus Box: If there are 10 red and blue jelly beans, how many of each color could there be? On the back of this sheet, show two different answers.

Jumbled Jelly Beans

Write the word below each picture.
Use the Word Bank.
Color each jelly bean after you use it.

Word Bank

chain
tie
leaf
boat
soap
jeep
rain

Bonus Box: On the back of this sheet, write a sentence with each of these words.

28 Name _____

A Graph Of Goodies

Color.
Count the jelly beans. Write the totals.
Finish the graph.

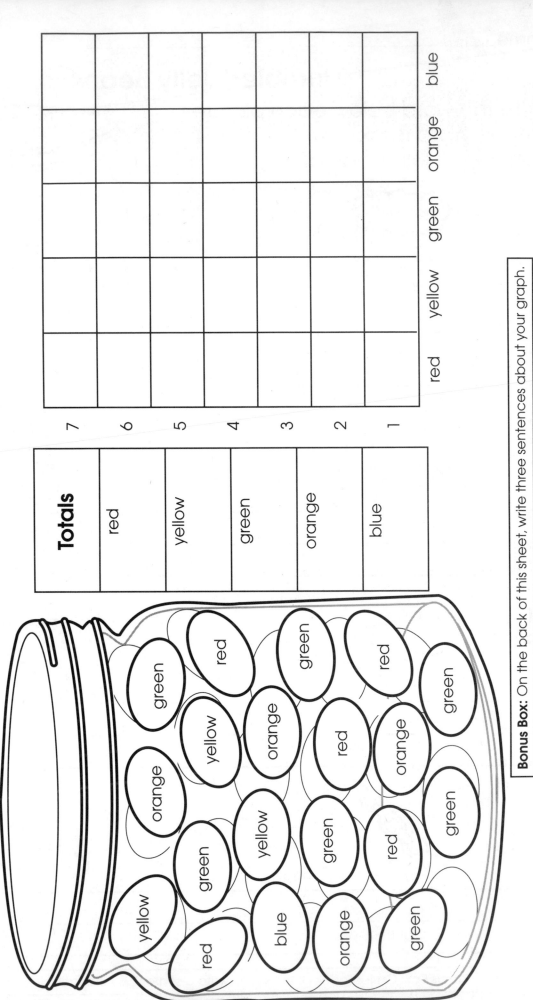

Totals	
red	
yellow	
green	
orange	
blue	

7
6
5
4
3
2
1

red   yellow   green   orange   blue

Bonus Box: On the back of this sheet, write three sentences about your graph.

BUNNY BASICS

With spring thriving and Easter arriving it's the perfect time to hop into a unit about bunnies! These adorable rabbits will have your students bounding into some basic skills practice.

Bunches Of Bunnies
Name _Ben_
Cut. Glue the words in ABC order.

basket	candy	egg	fun	grass
hunt	kids	paint	rabbit	spring

Bunny ABCs

Incorporate these lovable bunnies into any alphabetical order practice. Make one photocopy of page 31 and program the boxes at the bottom with ten words to be alphabetized. Choose rabbit- or Easter-related words, or focus on vocabulary that you're using currently in your classroom. Then photocopy a class supply of the programmed page. Have each child cut out the word cards, put them in order on the numbered boxes, and glue them in place. For plenty of alphabetizing practice, use this page again and again with different words.

Rabbit Writing

After investigating bunnies through books and other resources, your students will be eager to share what they know about these cute critters. Give each child a sheet of writing paper and suggest a story starter (there are several listed below). After each child completes her story, provide her with a copy of page 33. Have her cut along the heavy solid outline and glue the cutout along the top edge of her story as shown on the reproducible. What a perfect way to top off these rabbit writings!

Bunny Tale Beginnings

- One day a rabbit hopped into my garden.
- If a rabbit could talk, I think it would tell me…
- When the weather gets cold, rabbits…
- My rabbit likes to eat…
- My bunny leaped *so* high that it…
- I know a bunny that likes to read books about…

Name _____

All Ears

Look at each pair of words.
Color the circle beside the correct spelling.
Cut and glue to match the pictures.

○ chain
○ chayn

○ hai
○ hay

○ paint
○ paynt

○ rain
○ rayn

○ plai
○ play

○ craion
○ crayon

○ snail
○ snayl

○ nail
○ nayl

○ train
○ trayn

○ sprai
○ spray

Name _____

Bunches Of Bunnies

Cut. Glue the words in ABC order.

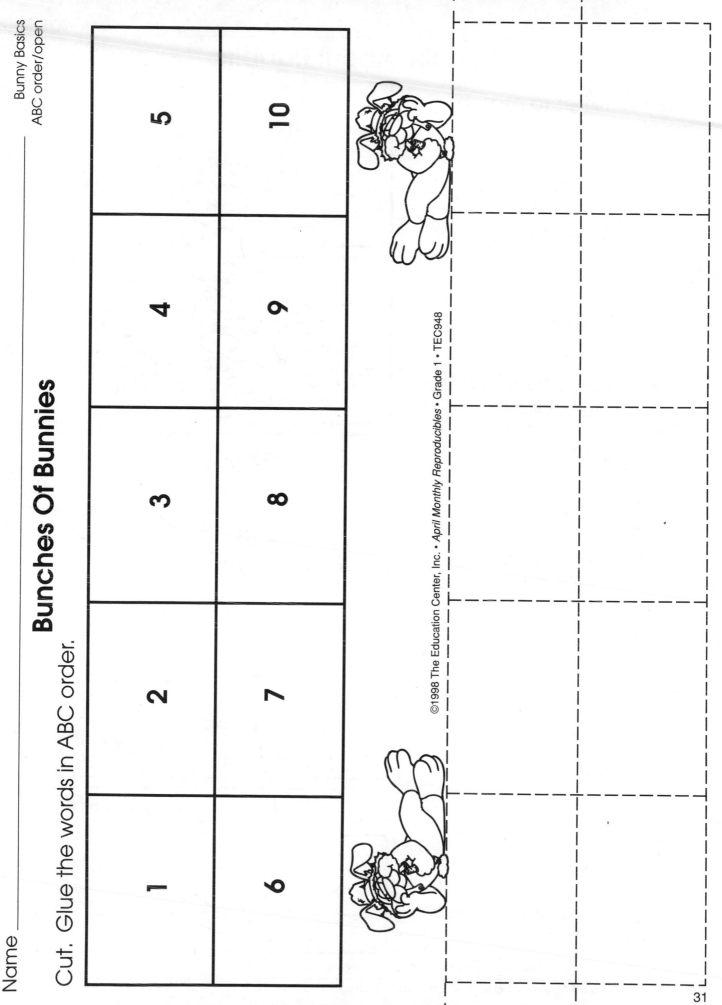

1	2	3	4	5
6	7	8	9	10

Readin' About Rabbits

Write the letter to match each fact to a picture.

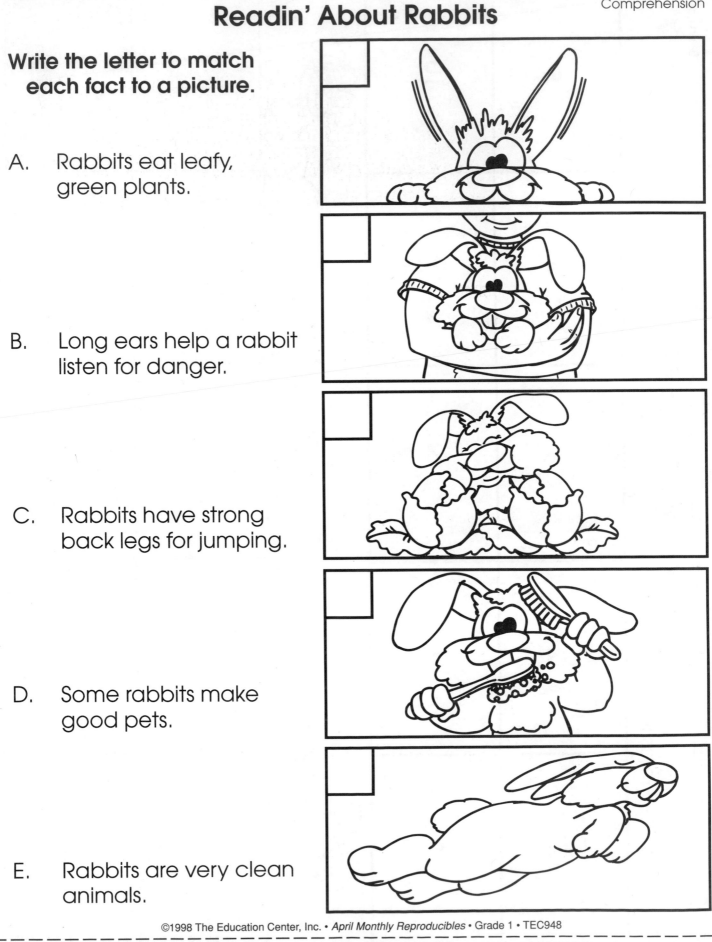

A. Rabbits eat leafy, green plants.

B. Long ears help a rabbit listen for danger.

C. Rabbits have strong back legs for jumping.

D. Some rabbits make good pets.

E. Rabbits are very clean animals.

Bunny Tales

Listen and do.

Finished Sample

©1998 The Education Center, Inc. • *April Monthly Reproducibles* • Grade 1 • TEC948

Note To The Teacher: Use with "Rabbit Writing" on page 29.

33

Name _____

Bunny's Delight

Add or subtract.

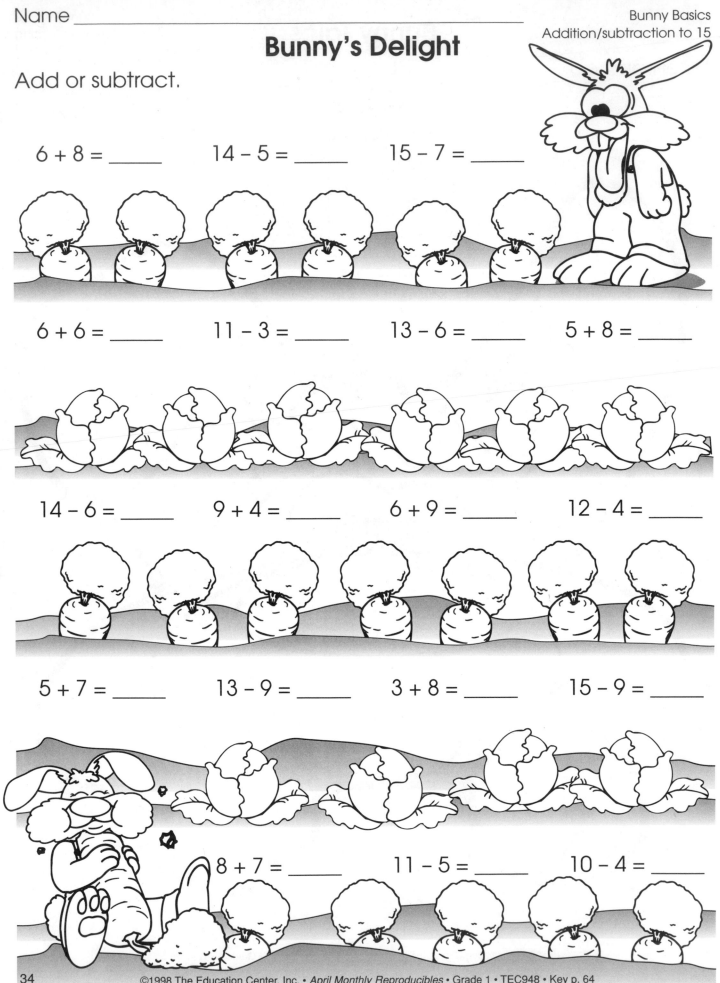

$6 + 8 =$ _____ $14 - 5 =$ _____ $15 - 7 =$ _____

$6 + 6 =$ _____ $11 - 3 =$ _____ $13 - 6 =$ _____ $5 + 8 =$ _____

$14 - 6 =$ _____ $9 + 4 =$ _____ $6 + 9 =$ _____ $12 - 4 =$ _____

$5 + 7 =$ _____ $13 - 9 =$ _____ $3 + 8 =$ _____ $15 - 9 =$ _____

$8 + 7 =$ _____ $11 - 5 =$ _____ $10 - 4 =$ _____

"EGG-CELLENT" EGGS

The first signs of spring lead us to think of hatching eggs. Are they all they're cracked up to be? From a home for a developing animal to a delicious treat to eat, share the wonders and benefits of the egg with your students during this "egg-stra-special" unit.

"Egg-stra" Information

Eggs can be fascinating! Not only do they vary greatly in size, color, and shape, but they also vary according to what hatches from them. Nearly all animals produce eggs. Reptiles' eggs have soft, waterproof shells. Amphibians, such as toads and frogs, lay eggs that have no shells at all—they are surrounded with a jellylike mass. Birds and insects lay eggs that have hard shells, while most mammals produce eggs that develop inside the mother's body.

Look What's Developing!

Help your students explore the contents of a chicken's egg. Crack an egg open on a plate so that students can examine the variety of its contents, such as the shell, membranes, yolk, and albumen. Explain that an egg used for cooking or baking was not *incubated* or kept warm so a chick never developed inside. If the egg had been incubated, however, a chick would have developed from the embryo on the yolk. Each of the egg parts would have served an important function in the chick's development. Give each child a copy of page 36. Have each student follow along on his paper as you discuss each part of the egg. Have each student follow these steps to create his own cross section of an egg.

Creating An Egg Cross Section
Each child should complete these steps:
1. Cut out the shell. Glue it to a 6" x 9" sheet of colored construction paper.
2. Color the outer membrane orange. Color the inner membrane pink. Cut out the membranes along the outermost line. Center the membrane cutout on the shell cutout and glue in place.
3. Color the air pocket blue; leave the albumen white. Cut out the albumen and air pocket along the outermost line. Center the cutout on the membranes and glue in place.
4. Color the yolk yellow; color the embryo red. Cut out the yolk on the outermost line. Center the cutout on the albumen and glue in place.
5. Cut out the fact box. Glue it to the blank side of the colored construction paper.

35

Colorful Cross Section

Listen and do.

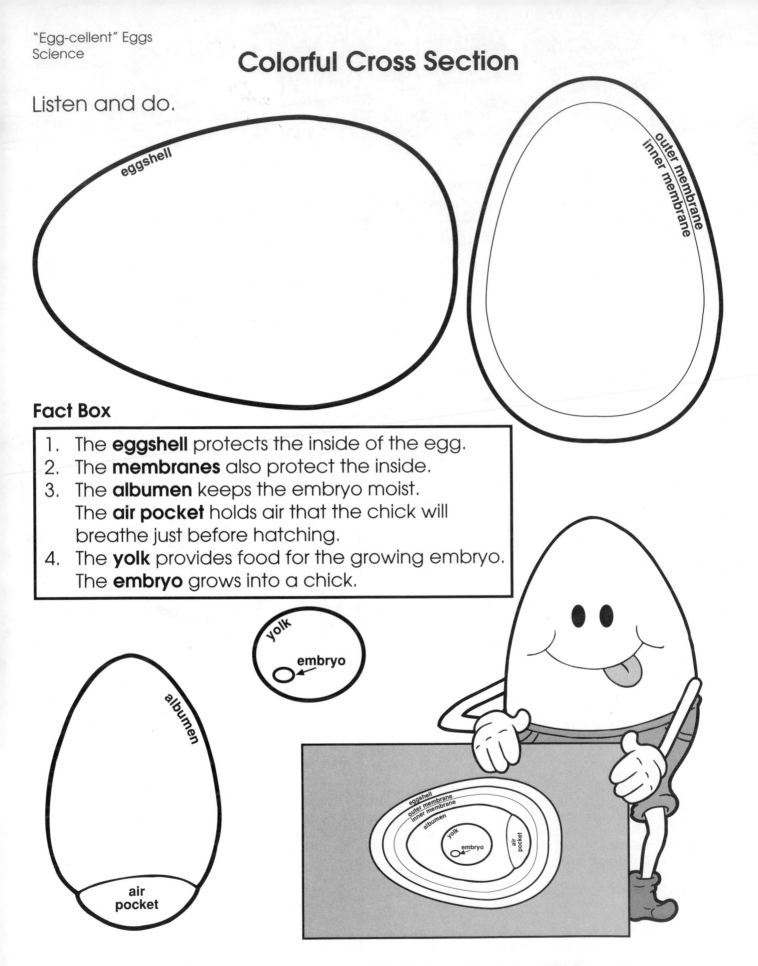

eggshell

outer membrane
inner membrane

Fact Box

1. The **eggshell** protects the inside of the egg.
2. The **membranes** also protect the inside.
3. The **albumen** keeps the embryo moist.
   The **air pocket** holds air that the chick will breathe just before hatching.
4. The **yolk** provides food for the growing embryo.
   The **embryo** grows into a chick.

yolk

embryo

albumen

air
pocket

eggshell
outer membrane
inner membrane
albumen
yolk
embryo
air
pocket

About To Hatch

The letter **y** can be a vowel.
It can make a long **i** sound or a long **e** sound.

Read each word.
Listen to the sound the **y** makes.
Color the egg half that shows the **y** sound.

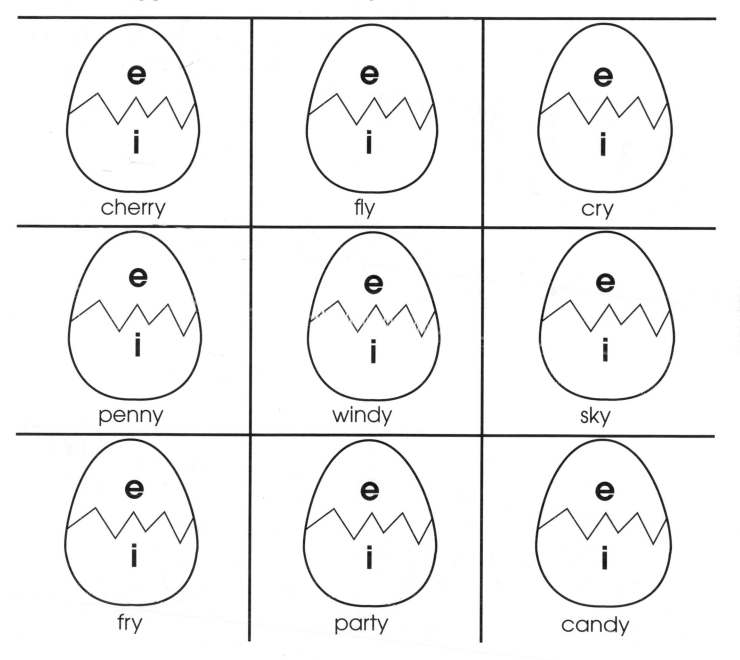

e / i **cherry**	e / i **fly**	e / i **cry**
e / i **penny**	e / i **windy**	e / i **sky**
e / i **fry**	e / i **party**	e / i **candy**

Sunny-Side Up!

Write **ar**, **ir**, or **or** to complete each word.
Color each yolk by the code.

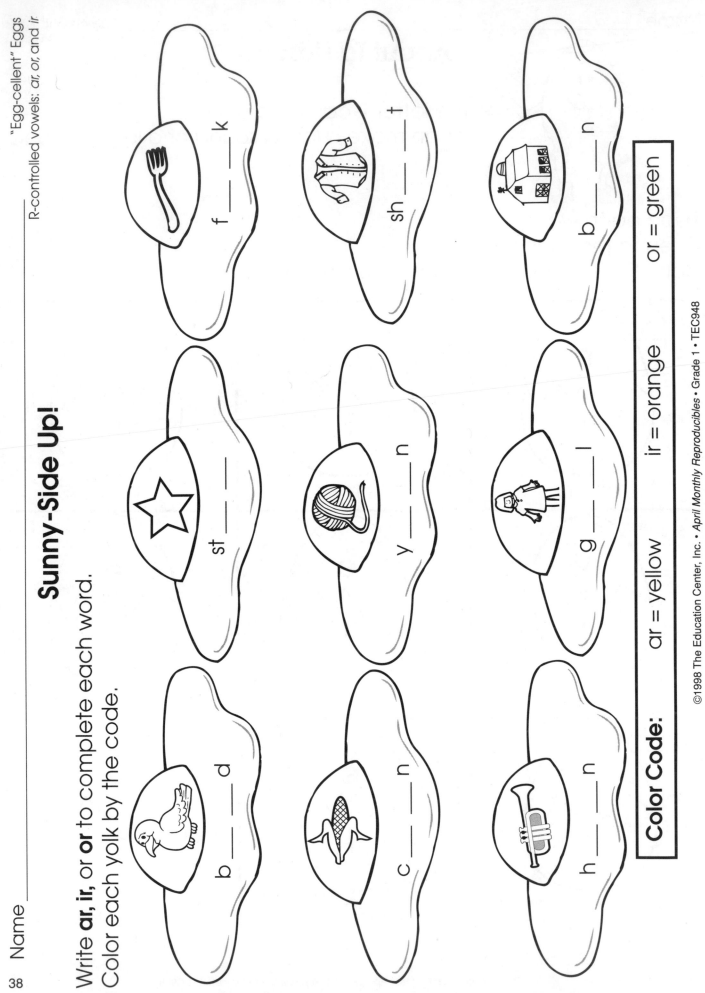

f __ __ k

sh __ __ t

b __ __ n

st __ __

y __ __ n

g __ __ l

b __ __ d

c __ __ n

h __ __ n

Color Code: ar = yellow   ir = orange   or = green

Name _____

A Good Egg

Name each picture.
Does it have a long or short vowel sound? Color.

duck	cake	pig
ŭ ū	ă ā	ĭ ī

mop	feet	cube	hose
ŏ ō	ĕ ē	ŭ ū	ŏ ō

bed	hat	kite	tent
ĕ ē	ă ā	ĭ ī	ĕ ē

tie	sun	flute	boat
ĭ ī	ŭ ū	ŭ ū	ŏ ō

Note To The Teacher: Have each child color a box below each picture to indicate the correct vowel sound.

Name_____

Scrambled Eggs

Cut. Glue each egg half to complete each problem.

+ 4
___
9

+ 6
___
13

+ 8
___
11

+ 5
___
15

+ 4
___
13

+ 6
___
12

+ 9
___
13

+ 6
___
14

+ 9
___
14

+ 7
___
9

+ 7
___
10

+ 7
___
15

10   7   6   3

9   4   5   5

2   3   8   8

Foster a love of literature and an appreciation of libraries with this important celebration! National Library Week is usually observed during the second week of April and recognizes one of our most useful institutions. Where else can you find books about any topic imaginable, magazines, newspapers, computers, maps, videotapes, and countless other media materials? Be sure to visit your local public library with students this week. Youngsters will have volumes of fun checking out all that it has to offer!

- April is National Library Month.

- April 2 is International Children's Book Day. It is also the birthdate of Hans Christian Andersen, well-known author of more than 150 fairy tales.

- The first free public library in the United States opened on April 9, 1833.

- On April 24, 1800, the Library of Congress was established.

There'll Be Consequences!

Aunt Chip gives this warning about closing the town library in *Aunt Chip And The Great Triple Creek Dam Affair* by Patricia Polacco (The Putnam Publishing Group, 1996). Everyone in Triple Creek loves watching television so much that TV is the focus of their lives and reading is obsolete. Read this moving story to youngsters and then lead them in a discussion about the value of libraries and reading. Ask students to brainstorm ways that people use reading in their daily lives, such as reading recipes, street signs, and directions for assembling toys. Record students' ideas on a large book-shaped cutout or chart paper; then display the list on a classroom wall. No doubt students will heed Aunt Chip's warning and recognize the wonderful treasures that libraries hold!

All Aboard!

Full steam ahead for reading fun! Read aloud a favorite library book to students; then explain that each youngster will make a train picture to tell about the story. Give each student a copy of page 43, and have him write his name and the story elements on the corresponding train cars. (If desired ask youngsters to color their train cars. Be sure to caution students to leave their writing clearly visible.) Direct each child to cut out his train cars and glue them in line on a long sheet of paper. Then ask each student to use crayons to add details, such as tracks, trees, and buildings. Display students' completed work in the school library or your classroom. You can be sure that youngsters will have trainloads of fun. Plus their story re-telling skills will be right on track!

- Thank You School Librarian Day honors school librarians on April 15.

Read each page.
Color. Cut. Staple.

**A Visit To
The Library**

Name _____

©1998 The Education Center, Inc.

Find a good book to read.
Check it out. **1**

Read it with clean hands. **2**

Use a bookmark. Keep the
pages of the book flat. **3**

Return the book on time. **4**

Look for more great
books! **5**

All Aboard!

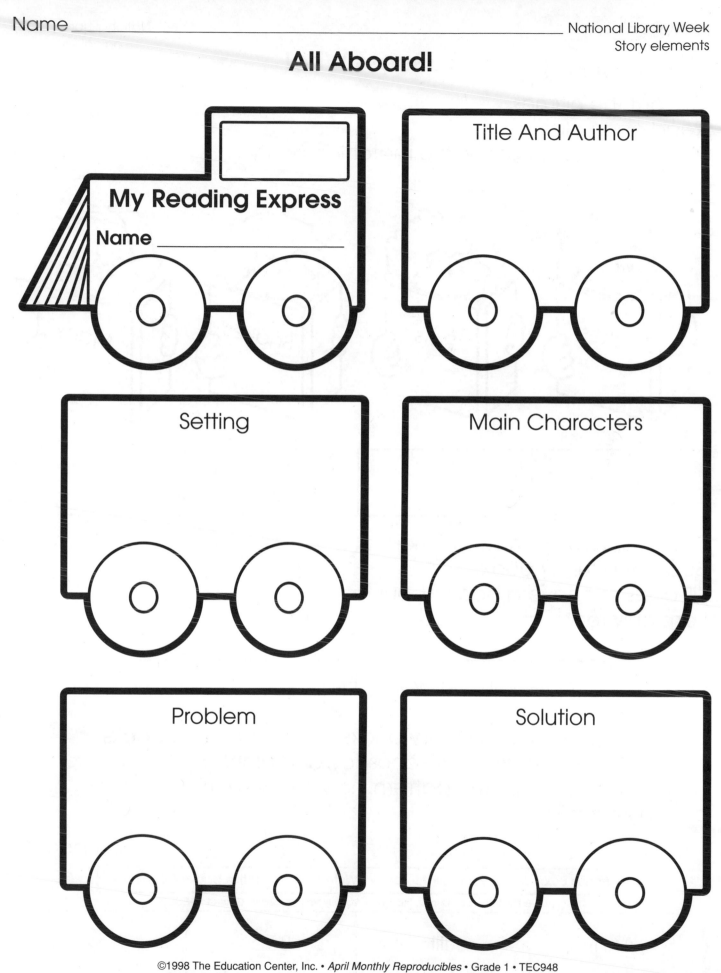

My Reading Express

Name _____

Title And Author

Setting

Main Characters

Problem

Solution

Note To The Teacher: Use with "All Aboard!" on page 41.

Guess Who!

Cut out the names.
Read each clue.
Glue each name below the matching person.

Jokes   Pets   Snakes   Maps

Ann has a book about animals.
Bob has a funny book.
Jill does not have a book about animals or jokes.
Sam only reads about snakes.

Read. Solve. Write your answer in the box.

Dan checked out two library books on Monday, four books
on Tuesday, six books on Wednesday, and eight books on
Thursday. If he keeps this pattern, how many will he check
out on Friday?

☐ books

Bonus Box: What is your favorite book? Write about it on the back of this sheet.

Ann   Jill   Bob   Sam

Cover Story

Synonyms are words that have the same meaning.

Read each pair of words.
If the words are synonyms, color the book yellow.
If they are **not** synonyms, color the book orange.

happy | glad

open | close

pig | hog

down | up

little | small

fast | quick

see | look

long | short

big | large

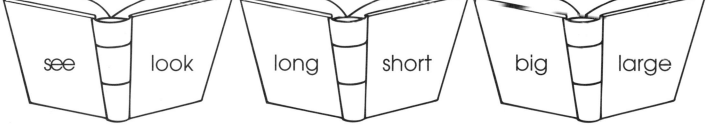

mail | send

say | tell

walk | skip

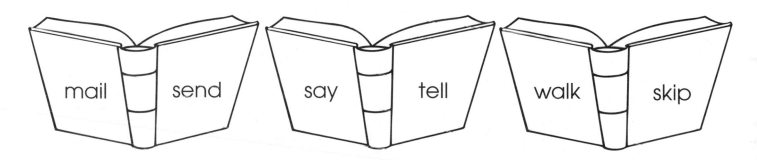

Bonus Box: Choose two synonym pairs. Write a sentence with each word on the back of this sheet.

A Batch Of Books

Antonyms are words that have opposite meanings.

Write each antonym below the matching book.
Use the Word Bank.

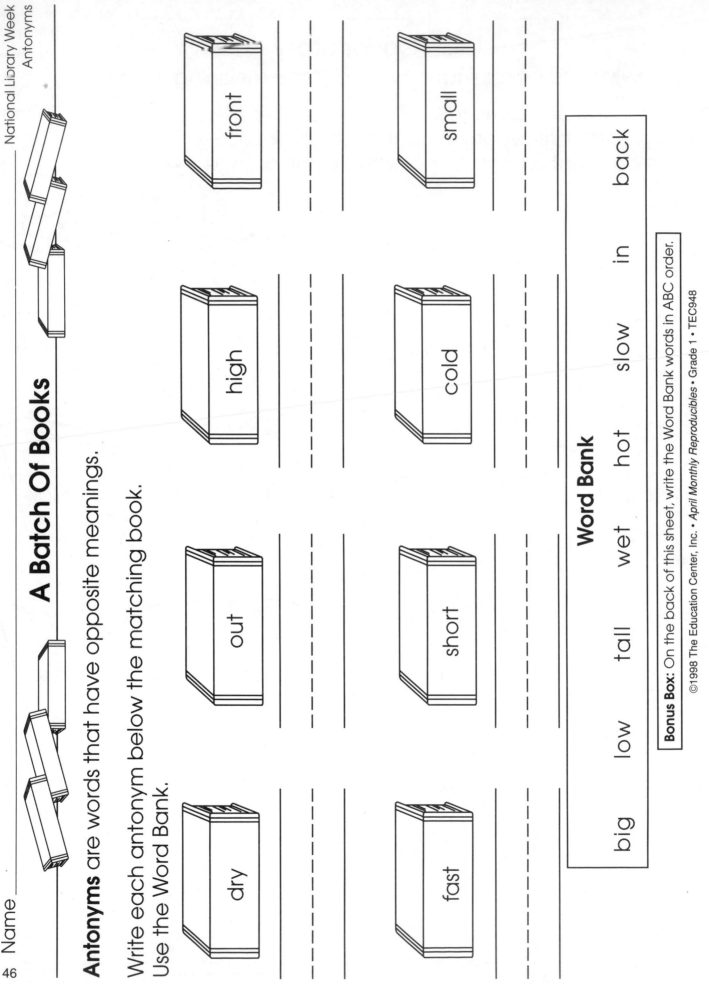

dry _____

out _____

high _____

front _____

fast _____

short _____

cold _____

small _____

Word Bank

big   low   tall   wet   hot   slow   in   back

Bonus Box: On the back of this sheet, write the Word Bank words in ABC order.

BASEBALL AT ITS BEST!

On April 14, 1910, President William Howard Taft started a sports tradition by throwing out the first baseball of the season, helping to make the game a national pastime. So start your own tradition by bringing baseball into your classroom with this delightful unit!

A BIT ABOUT BASEBALL

Here's a brief look at baseball basics. Baseball is played between two teams of nine players each. The playing area is a large field with four bases that mark the route a player must run to score. The teams take turns batting (offense) and fielding (defense). To put the ball in play, a pitcher from the fielding team throws the ball to a batter. The batter tries to hit the ball—using a bat—toward the opponents in the field. By hitting the ball, and by other means, the batter gets a chance to run to each of the bases. While the batter is running, the fielding team tries a variety of techniques to get the batting team out. But if the batter successfully reaches all four bases, he scores a run for his team. When the team at bat has three outs, they become the fielders. When each team has been at bat and in the field, an inning is complete. The team with the most runs after nine innings wins the game.

BATTER UP!

Students will be ready to step up to bat with this handy management system for learning centers or other independent activities. Create a form similar to the one shown and photocopy a class supply. Program the bases on each child's form with independent activities to be completed. As each child completes the activities in order from first base to home plate, he colors in the related bases. After all four activities have been finished, award each child with a home-run prize.

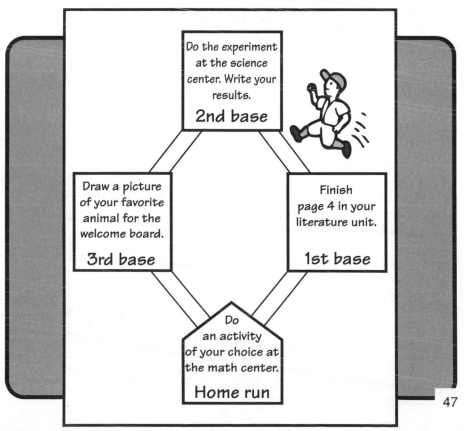

Do the experiment at the science center. Write your results.
2nd base

Draw a picture of your favorite animal for the welcome board.
3rd base

Finish page 4 in your literature unit.
1st base

Do an activity of your choice at the math center.
Home run

Facts At Bat

Read the sentence on each bat.
Color each bat. Use the code.

Color Code	
fact = brown	opinion = orange

Baseball is played on a field.

Baseball is fun to play.

A baseball is hit with a bat.

Baseball is played with two teams.

A baseball game lasts nine innings.

You should sing during a game.

Hitting a baseball is hard work.

The batting team is out after three strikes.

Bonus Box: Write your **opinion** of baseball on the back of this sheet.

Note To The Teacher: Review some baseball information with your students before they complete this page. See "A Bit About Baseball" on page 47.

Who's Winning?

Scoreboard

Inning	1	2	3	4	5	6	7	8	9	Total Runs
Bats	0	2	1	3	0	2	1	0	2	
Stars	1	0	1	0	2	1	3	0	4	

Answer each question.
Use the scoreboard.

1. Which team scored the most runs in the 4th inning? _____

2. Which team scored 2 runs in the 5th inning? _____

3. How many runs did the Bats score in the 2nd inning? _____

4. How many runs did the Stars score in the 5th inning? _____

5. In what inning did both teams score 1 run? _____

6. How many runs did the Bats score in innings 1 and 2? _____

Bonus Box: Add each team's scores for all nine innings. Write the total score for each team at the end of the scoreboard. Circle the winning team's name on the scoreboard.

Fly Ball

Read the word on each baseball.
For each compound word, write the two words that form it.
If a word is not compound, put an X on the word.

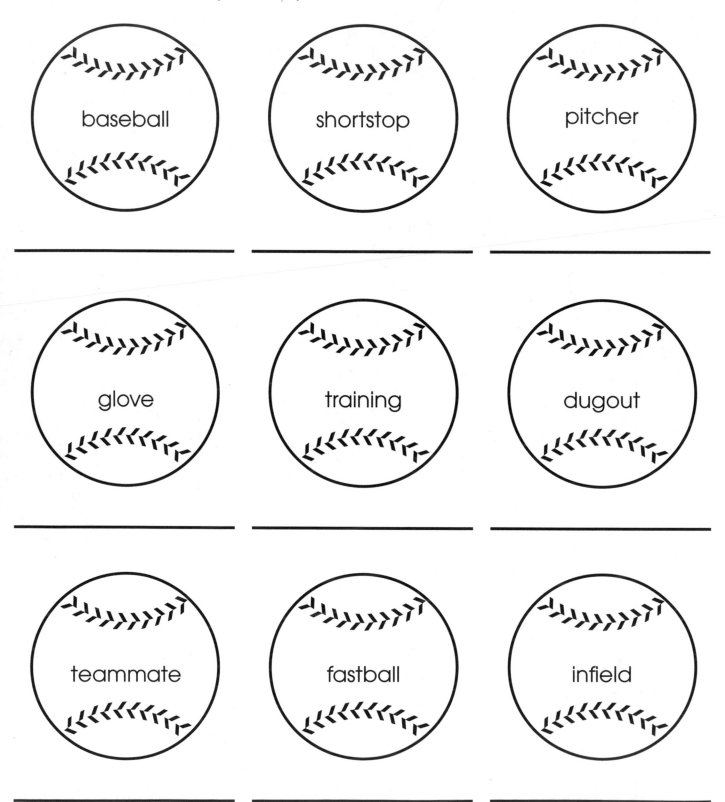

baseball

shortstop

pitcher

glove

training

dugout

teammate

fastball

infield

Name_____

Batter Up!

Say each word.
Listen for syllables.
Write the number of syllables beside
     each word.

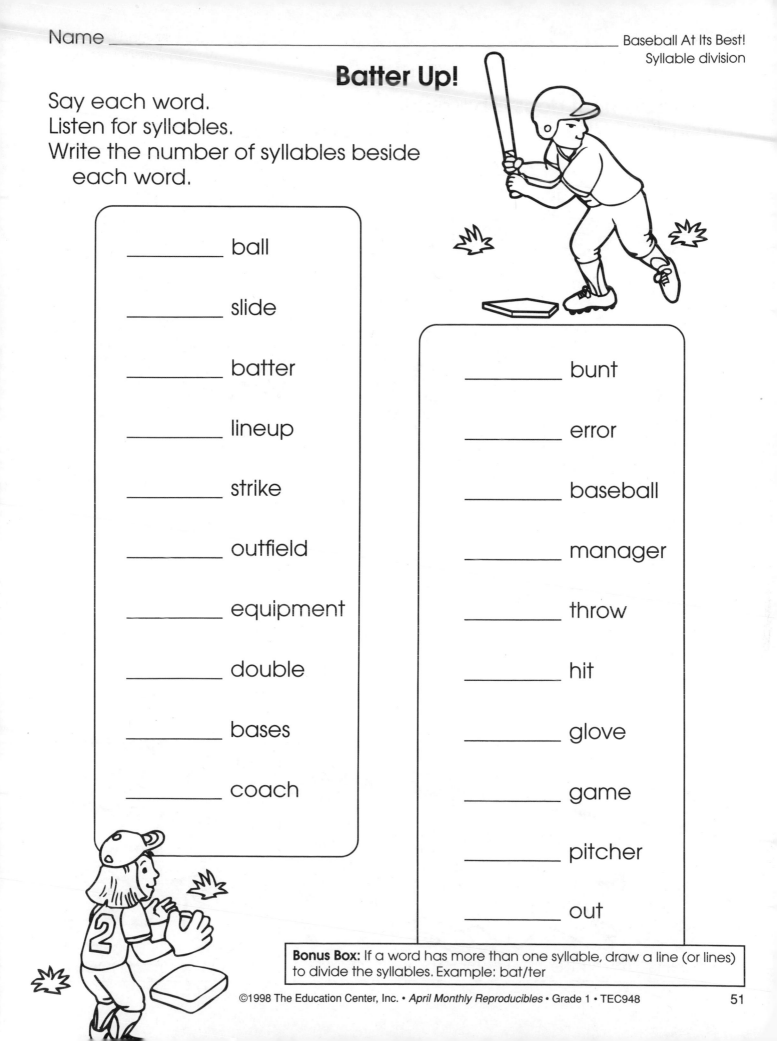

_____ ball	_____ bunt
_____ slide	_____ error
_____ batter	_____ baseball
_____ lineup	_____ manager
_____ strike	_____ throw
_____ outfield	_____ hit
_____ equipment	_____ glove
_____ double	_____ game
_____ bases	_____ pitcher
_____ coach	_____ out

Bonus Box: If a word has more than one syllable, draw a line (or lines)
to divide the syllables. Example: bat/ter

Suit Up

What equipment does a baseball player need?
Cut and glue the correct items around the player.

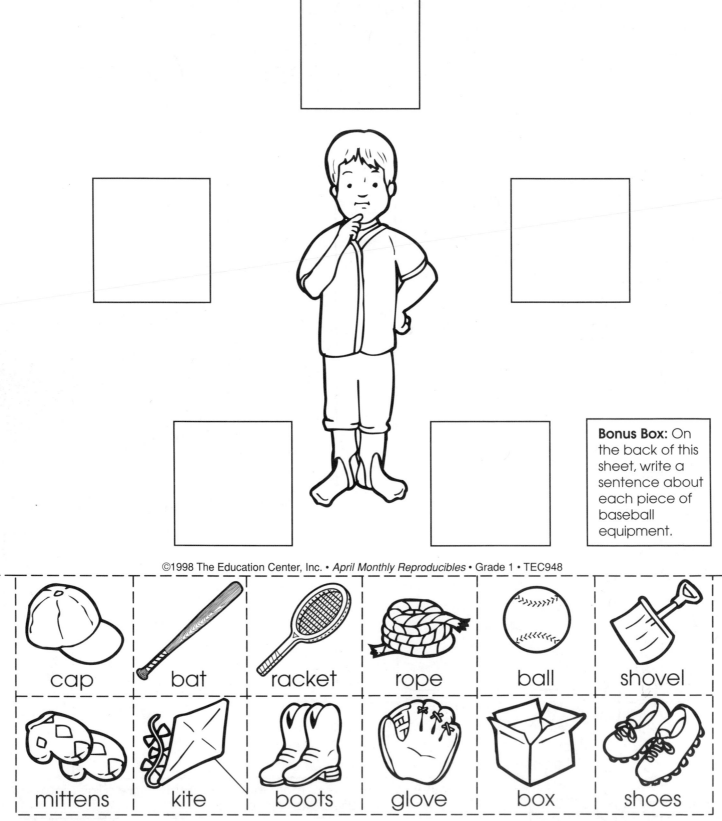

Bonus Box: On the back of this sheet, write a sentence about each piece of baseball equipment.

cap	bat	racket	rope	ball	shovel
mittens	kite	boots	glove	box	shoes

Our Fine-Feathered Friends

Student learning will soar with this "egg-citing" unit about birds! There are approximately 9,000 different kinds of birds, ranging from large flightless ostriches to tiny hummingbirds that can fly forward, backward, upside down, and can even turn somersaults in the air. Many differences exist among birds, but they have one distinguishing feature in common: feathers, or *plumage*. No other animals bear this trait.

Birds keep their feathers in good condition by *preening,* a process of smoothing and cleaning their feathers. When a bird loses a feather, a new one grows in its place. Birds lose and replace their feathers regularly. This process is called *molting*. Many male birds have very colorful feathers to attract mates. In contrast, most female birds have drab feathers to camouflage them in their nests and protect them from predators.

Give youngsters a bird's-eye view of this background information; then have some high-flying fun with these related facts and activities!

In Peru a bridge known as The Bridge of Eggs was built in 1610 with a mixture of mortar and 10,000 egg whites.

The largest bird is the male African ostrich, which grows approximately 8 feet tall. The smallest bird is the bee hummingbird. This bird is about 2 inches tall when it is fully grown.

Crocodile birds fly into crocodiles' mouths and eat the food left around their teeth.

Some swans have more than 25,000 feathers. In contrast, some hummingbirds have fewer than 1,000.

Hummingbirds have the fastest wing beats of all birds: 80 flaps per second.

What's For Lunch?

A hungry cat is tired of mild lunches and sets off in search of something more tasty in Lois Ehlert's *Feathers For Lunch* (Harcourt Brace & Company, 1996). Read aloud this delightful rhyming story; then share the information about birds provided at the end of the book. Invite each youngster to name his favorite type of bird and to explain why he likes it. Then have each child create an illustration of his bird with watercolor paints or colored paper, using Ehlert's collage technique as a model. Display students' completed pictures on a brightly colored bulletin board titled "The Best In The Nest." No doubt students' creativity will take flight with this engaging project!

A Flock Of Facts

Read each sentence.
Write **F** beside each fact.
Write **O** beside each opinion.

1. Birds are pretty. _____

2. Birds are animals. _____

3. Birds have feathers. _____

4. Bird songs sound silly. _____

5. Birds hatch from eggs. _____

6. Birds are the best pets. _____

7. Some birds have hooked beaks. _____

8. Birds can grow new feathers. _____

9. Baby birds are cute. _____

10. Some birds do not fly. _____

Bonus Box: On the back of this sheet, write three more facts about birds.

Whose Nests?

Cut.
Glue each nest below the matching bird.

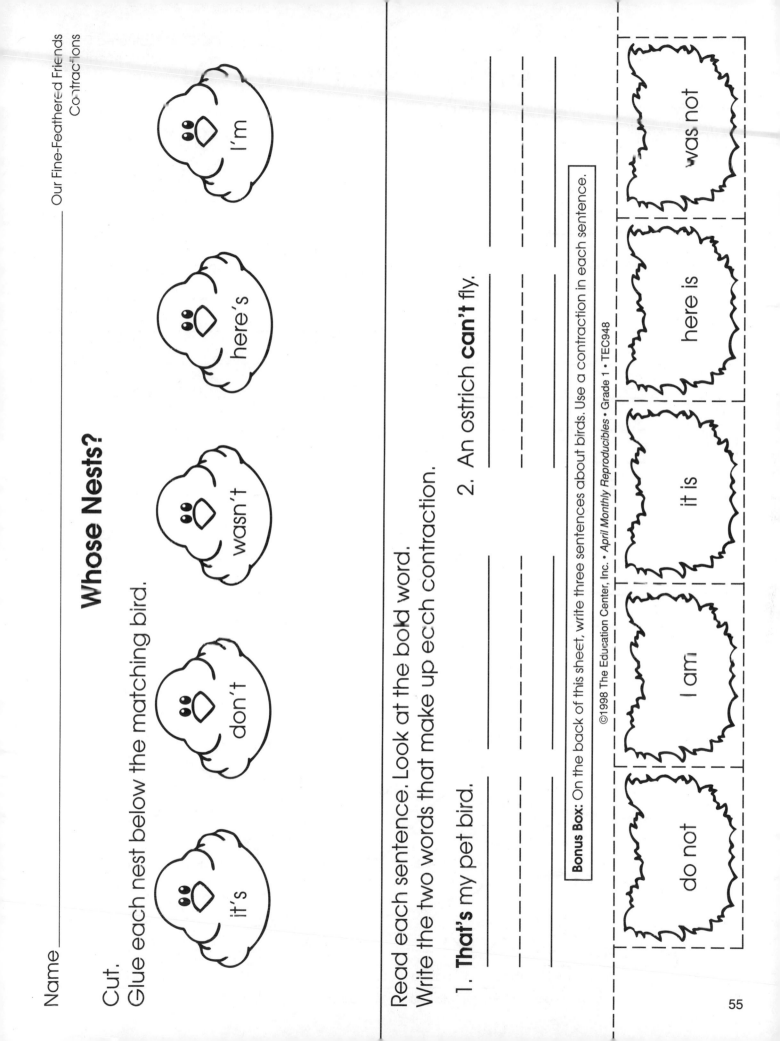

I'm

here's

wasn't

don't

it's

Read each sentence. Look at the bold word.
Write the two words that make up each contraction.

1. **That's** my pet bird.

_____ _____

2. An ostrich **can't** fly.

_____ _____

Bonus Box: On the back of this sheet, write three sentences about birds. Use a contraction in each sentence.

was not

here is

it is

I am

do not

An "Egg-cellent" Nest

Write the words in ABC order.
Color each egg when you use it.

1. _____

_ _ _ _ _ _ _ _ _ _ _ _ _ _

_____

2. _____

_ _ _ _ _ _ _ _ _ _ _ _ _ _

_____

3. _____

_ _ _ _ _ _ _ _ _ _ _ _ _ _

_____

4. _____

_ _ _ _ _ _ _ _ _ _ _ _ _ _

_____

5. _____

_ _ _ _ _ _ _ _ _ _ _ _ _ _

_____

6. _____

_ _ _ _ _ _ _ _ _ _ _ _ _ _

_____

7. _____

_ _ _ _ _ _ _ _ _ _ _ _ _ _

_____

8. _____

_ _ _ _ _ _ _ _ _ _ _ _ _ _

_____

9. _____

_ _ _ _ _ _ _ _ _ _ _ _ _ _

_____

10. _____

_ _ _ _ _ _ _ _ _ _ _ _ _ _

_____

egg   fly   robin   wing   ostrich   hatch   nest   beak   duck   sing

Bonus Box: On the back of this sheet, draw a picture of your favorite kind of bird. Write about it.

Mathematics Education Month

Whether you're at home, at school, in a park, or in a store, you'll discover math. Each year this important subject is featured in a monthlong celebration by the National Council of Teachers of Mathematics. Join this celebration by teaching youngsters about the importance of math in their daily lives and engaging them in a variety of exciting math activities. Youngsters will soon learn that math really counts!

Ready, Set, Roll!

It will be a race to the finish with this fast-paced addition game! Give each student a copy of page 62. Explain that the goal of this game is to be the first player to color each section of his racetrack, from the starting line to the finish line. Divide youngsters into groups of two or three, and give each group a pair of numeral dice and crayons. To play, each child, in turn, rolls the dice, adds the numerals shown, and announces the total. The child who rolls the greatest sum in each group colors one space on his gameboard. If two youngsters in a group roll the same total, those two roll again and the player who then has the greater sum colors two spaces. Play continues in a like manner until one youngster crosses the finish line. Now that's "sum" math game!

What A Difference!

From store owners who track inventory and determine profits, to children who calculate how much time is left before their favorite television show, people of all ages and lifestyles use math daily. Help youngsters realize the importance of math with this fun investigation. Have each child interview a familiar adult in the community, at school, or at home to find out how he uses math. After every child has interviewed someone, invite youngsters to share their information with the class. Record their findings on a chart titled "Math Makes A Difference" and post it in your classroom to serve as a handy reminder of this valuable lesson.

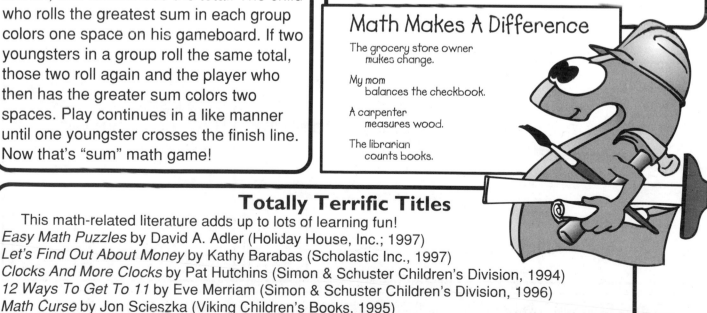

Math Makes A Difference

The grocery store owner makes change.

My mom balances the checkbook.

A carpenter measures wood.

The librarian counts books.

Totally Terrific Titles

This math-related literature adds up to lots of learning fun!

Easy Math Puzzles by David A. Adler (Holiday House, Inc.; 1997)
Let's Find Out About Money by Kathy Barabas (Scholastic Inc., 1997)
Clocks And More Clocks by Pat Hutchins (Simon & Schuster Children's Division, 1994)
12 Ways To Get To 11 by Eve Merriam (Simon & Schuster Children's Division, 1996)
Math Curse by Jon Scieszka (Viking Children's Books, 1995)
Right In Your Own Backyard: Nature Math edited by Elizabeth Ward et al. (Time-Life, Inc.; 1992)

Name_____

Playground Puzzlers

Read each box.
Add or subtract.
Write the answer.

5 children are swinging. 2 stop. How many are left swinging? ☐	7 children are playing ball. 2 more play. How many in all? ☐	3 boys are swinging. 6 girls are playing tag. How many children in all? ☐
3 girls are playing ball. 3 boys are playing ball. How many children in all? ☐	10 children are playing tag. 7 stop. How many are left playing tag? ☐	3 children are jumping rope. 5 children are playing ball. How many children in all? ☐
8 children are playing ball. 3 stop playing. How many are left playing ball? ☐	4 boys are swinging. 3 girls are swinging. How many children in all? ☐	6 children are playing. 4 go inside. How many are left playing? ☐

Bonus Box: On the back of this sheet, write two more playground story problems.

It's About Time!

Complete each sentence.
Draw hands on each clock to match.

My Day

I wake up
at ____:____.

I eat lunch
at ____:____.

I eat breakfast
at ____:____.

I go home
at ____:____.

I go to school
at ____:____.

I eat supper
at ____:____.

Write a sentence that tells what time you go to bed.
Draw hands on the clock to match.

_____

- -

_____

_____

- -

_____

Bonus Box: Draw a star beside each clock that shows a time before 2:00 P.M.

Note To The Teacher: If desired, introduce this activity by reading aloud *Get Up And Go!* by Stuart J. Murphy
(Scholastic Inc., 1996).

Shopping Spree

Count each set of coins.
Write each amount.
Cut.
Glue each item beside
the matching amount.

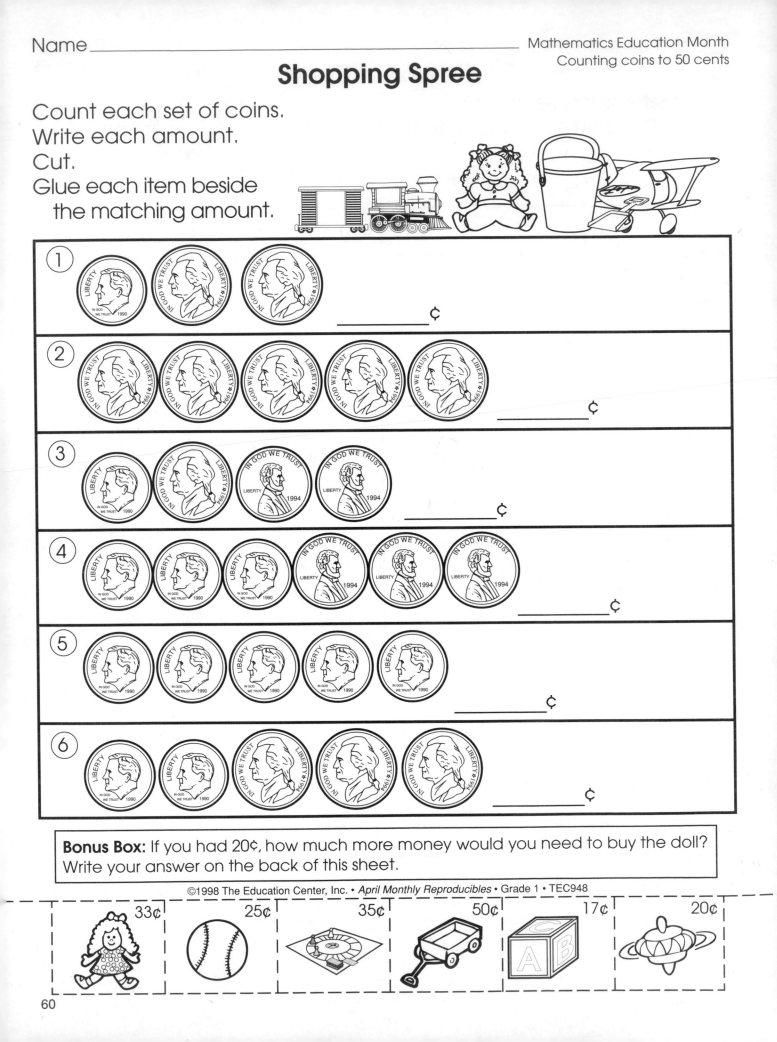

① _____¢

② _____¢

③ _____¢

④ _____¢

⑤ _____¢

⑥ _____¢

Bonus Box: If you had 20¢, how much more money would you need to buy the doll?
Write your answer on the back of this sheet.

33¢   25¢   35¢   50¢   17¢   20¢

Mark Your Calendar!

Complete the calendar.

April _____
year

Sunday	Monday	Tuesday	Wednesday	Thursday	Friday	Saturday

Answer the questions. Use the calendar.

What is the first day of the month?

_____

_____

What is the last day of the month?

_____

_____

Follow the directions.

Draw an **X** on each day that you do not have school.
Draw a ◯ on the second Wednesday.
Draw a ★ on the first Tuesday.

Ready, Set, Roll!

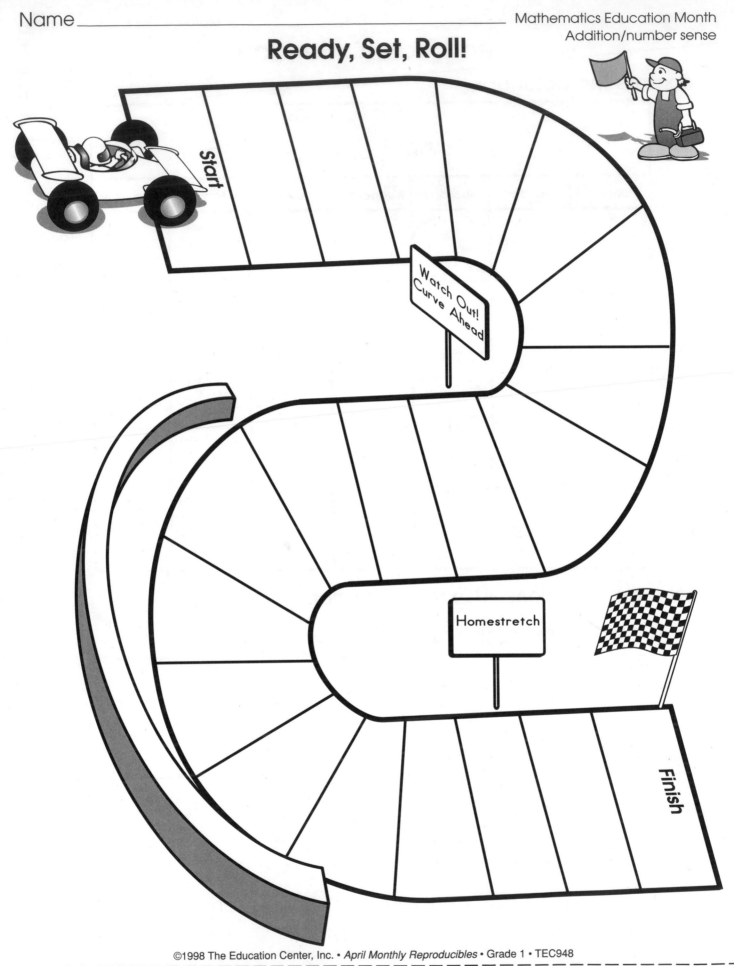

Start

Watch Out!
Curve Ahead

Homestretch

Finish

Name _____

Team Lineup

Cut.
Glue in order on the clothesline.

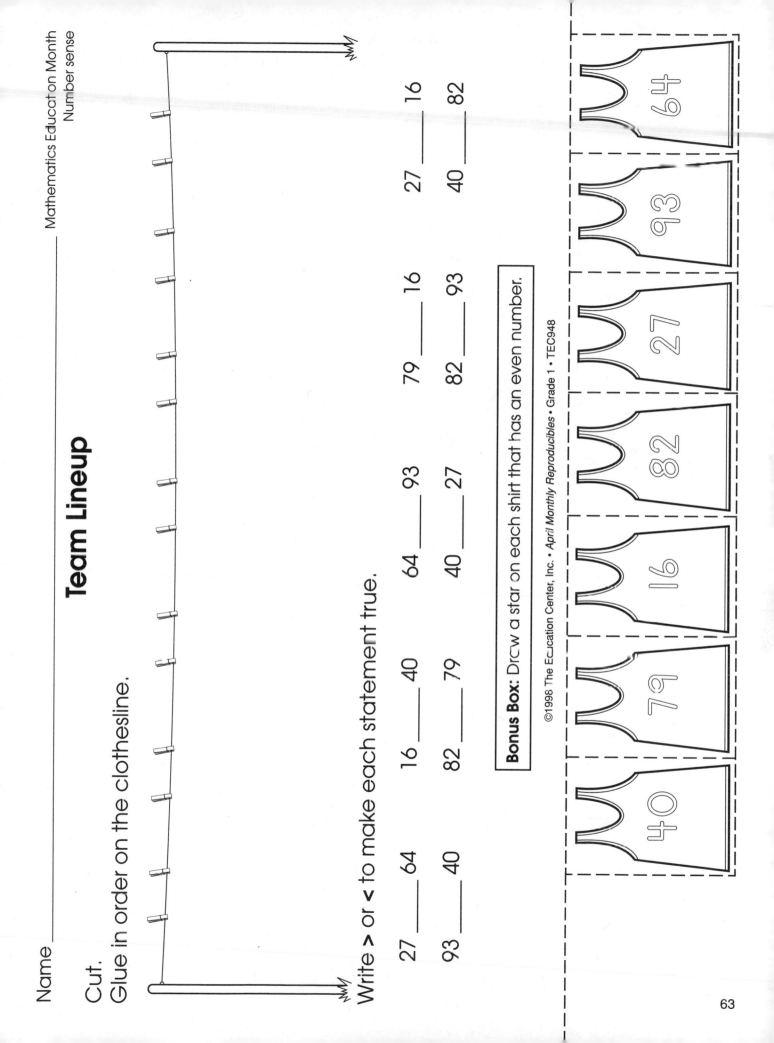

Write > or < to make each statement true.

27 ___ 64   16 ___ 40   64 ___ 93   79 ___ 16   27 ___ 16

93 ___ 40   82 ___ 79   40 ___ 27   82 ___ 93   40 ___ 82

Bonus Box: Draw a star on each shirt that has an even number.

64   93   27   82   16   79   40

Answer Keys

Page 6
1. Friday
2. 6 inches
3. Tuesday
4. Wednesday
5. Monday and Thursday
6. 18 inches

Page 7

Write each ⬭ letter.

d d e s p l u

Unscramble the letters to find out what rain makes. Write.

puddles

Page 10

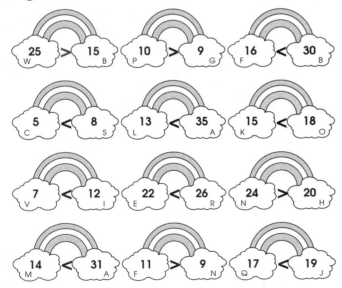

To solve the riddle, match the letters of the greater numbers to the lines. Some numbers will not be used.

What kind of bow is hard to tie?

A R A I N B O W
35 26 31 12 24 30 18 25

Page 23
1. Wood comes from trees.
2. Animals live in trees.
3. Trees give us shade.
4. Fruits grow on trees.
5. We make paper from trees.

Page 34

$6 + 8 = \underline{14}$ $14 - 5 = \underline{9}$ $15 - 7 = \underline{8}$

$6 + 6 = \underline{12}$ $11 - 3 = \underline{8}$ $13 - 6 = \underline{7}$ $5 + 8 = \underline{13}$

$14 - 6 = \underline{8}$ $9 + 4 = \underline{13}$ $6 + 9 = \underline{15}$ $12 - 4 = \underline{8}$

$5 + 7 = \underline{12}$ $13 - 9 = \underline{4}$ $3 + 8 = \underline{11}$ $15 - 9 = \underline{6}$

$8 + 7 = \underline{15}$ $11 - 5 = \underline{6}$ $10 - 4 = \underline{6}$

Page 54
1. O
2. F
3. F
4. O
5. F
6. O
7. F
8. F
9. O
10. F

Page 56
1. beak
2. duck
3. egg
4. fly
5. hatch
6. nest
7. ostrich
8. robin
9. sing
10. wing